The Night I Spoke Irish in Surrey

Richard Hawtree

The Night I Spoke Irish in Surrey

© Richard Hawtree
First Edition 2019
ISBN: 978-1-907435-75-1

Richard Hawtree has asserted his authorship and given his permission to Dempsey & Windle for these poems to be published here.

A CIP record for this book can be obtained from the British Library.

Published by Dempsey & Windle
15 Rosetrees
Guildford
Surrey
GU1 2HS
UK
01483 571164
dempseyandwindle.com

for John and Anna

Acknowledgements

I thank the editors of the following British and Irish literary magazines where some of these poems first appeared: *Tales from the Forest, The Stinging Fly, Crossways, Scintilla, A New Ulster, Banshee, Boyne Berries, Quarryman, SOUTH, Snakeskin Poetry, Anima, Brain of Forgetting, Poetry & All That Jazz, The Penny Dreadful, The Honest Ulsterman, The Weary Blues,* and *Weyfarers.*

'April Leaps' was first published as part of Limerick City's inaugural Poetry Trail in April 2016 and reprinted in *Poems to Keep* (D & W Publishing, 2017).

'The Night I Spoke Irish in Surrey' first appeared in the anthology *What the Elephant Said to the Peacock* (D & W Publishing, 2018).

Contents

April Leaps

April leaps from the city's lap,
all bird song and blossom on footpaths –
toddlers and trad musicians swerve,
rattle and bodhrán are swept
from quayside to castle
and back with a clack
as tides curl and diverge.
It doesn't matter if you call this spring,
Easter, Lent or vernal equinox:
April's fling will happen anyway
with you or someone else, so break the locks
and smoor the hearths and let spring sway

in both your wintry hips and linger where
the rhythm is strongest in the April air.

Space Walk

on the thirteenth-century Westminster Abbey pavement

Henry on his throne,
a blur of gold and dazzle.
What shall we create?

Marble freight from Rome
cut to Westminster shadows,
heaven's own pavement.

Sheer porphyry spheres
orbit Egyptian onyx,
freeze across comets.

Each raw universe
stretching its honed patina,
live with dark matter

while unflagging ochre dust
rings my eyes like henna
brushed on troubled skin.

Our space walk begins.

Helping Syllables

When the Sean Nós singers strayed northward
they added their own helping syllables
to each rime-dusted palace and Wi-Fi point.

So when they steered homeward in their top-heavy ship,
frothing with spirit and herring for ballast, those lithe
and glittering mariners saw this: a green light shifting

with lengthened tongues out in the archipelago. How they gazed
as each macron blade tip stirred the eddic waters of Stockholum.

The Mountain Calls Down

To set each stanza
limber on its feet, I sound
the drift of tanka,
swishing the stippled whooper-
swan currents while above us

the mountain calls down
to the valley: five, seven,
five, seven, seven –
until, lover, no tally
will ever fathom our beat.

Three Cork Haiku

Repositioned Fireplace, 1597

Down North Main Street, high
Above us a fireplace floats –
Excavated hearth.

Inverted Ship's Cannon, 1800

On the Grand Parade
A cannon sinks its muzzle
Deep into lost streams.

Modern Sheela-na-Gig, No Date

Way up Lavitt's quay
Her swift parting of stone thighs
Stuns the passing feet.

A Desert Master

i.m. Wallace Orr

'You were not shaped to live like beasts,
but to pursue knowledge and virtue.'
Dante, Inferno, xxvi, 119-20

Although not very taken with the saints,
on that last day in Ballyvourney
you placed your whole arm through Saint Gobnait's church wall
to reach the relic called her 'bowling ball':
revealing that an old man's heart has room
for miracles denied by David Hume.
You brought the farthest matter near to us,
praising the *Georgics* by a kitchen stove –

your hand retreating from that cavity,
now shades you in a distant apple grove
where you are reading Dante and your voice
arcs gently back to Munster:
knowledge and virtue plaited in your laughter,
rushes blessed by a desert master.

Night Thoughts

Shift

Get up at 3:00 a.m.
Devices charging. Check. The wireless night
shakes lightest dust out of an awkward eye:
the Perseids again.

Balance
from the Old Irish of Colmán of Cloyne

As balance tumbles back
after satire's sting,
so silver risks a smile
after polishing.

In Småland

When you were young, you said you wouldn't hold
her hand for all the butter in Småland.
Since your hands grew old, you hold each other
folded in the fickle, boreal nights.

A Better Lever

for Elizabeth Ilive (1769 –1822), mistress and, later, wife of the third earl of Egremont. In 1796 she invented an improved cross-bar lever at Petworth House, West Sussex.

You raised six children and commissioned two
watercolours from William Blake.
Expenditure included sums for flasks
dappled with tense experimental grains
of dawn-lit chemical. In other lights and moods
you walked the Petworth grounds, watching the servants sway
beneath the stoic marble orators.
High time, you said, to find a better lever

for raising busts of Cicero. So you invented one
(winning a silver medal from the men)
to stun your future husband's mistresses.
Even when the third earl married you
he never guessed how levers operate
inside enlightened minds to shift the weight.

Why Do You Wake the Sleeping Tear?

after fragments by Callimachus, The Aeneid XI, The Iliad XVIII

Diver gulls rise from the sea at noon,
dice skitter from the Libyan antelope –

only the canny nuthatch longs
for you to wake the sleeping tear.

*

Aeneas did things us schoolboys could not:
stripping an oak of branches to pin up
the shields of mangled enemies before
turning his step towards the pyre-red camp.

But what unnerved us most was his clear knack
for shedding tears, not blood; and when he wept
our freshly scanned hexameters grew hot
and, later, brittle with the sting of war.

*

A blackbird charged at the garden window –
grief's clang earthed the bronzed Achilles.
Still on the glass, the static of her wings.

Catullus Turns to Michael Hartnett

1 Pied-à-terre *from Catullus 68*

Allius gave us his assistance
turning trespass into open access:
he secured both maisonette and mistress,
a shared bolt-hole to school our eager loves.

Hear the deft tread of my flaring goddess
searing the threshold with her white hot foot
poised at our door, the urgent tinnitus
of her quick sandal sprang across the house.

2 Love / Hate *after Catullus 85*

I love and hate –

clear causes why
I cannot yet articulate.

And even as you gently slide
into my mixed-up state –

we're crucified.

3   **A Poet's Road**   *after Hartnett's An Phurgóid*

When roads are purged of their milestones
and lovers lack rambling-houses,

shy herbs will still come billowing
from every sullen verge.

Stray Versicles

I *after Colmán of Cloyne*

I do not wake to a weak stanza
after lush and dream rich sleep:

my verse is rest from a Lenten fast,
grace distilled from Christ's own cask.

II *after the Anglo-Saxon Guthlac poet*

That is the turning of love's gates
when in our hearts she elevates

those gifts of spirit.
Even her master bids us drink –

to think
and let love sink

right through –
making our hinges new.

III *on an Irish psalter raised from Faddan More bog*

So up with you then illuminated bird
singing a new psalm from soft Faddan More,

your plumage stiffened with ink,
your hooked beak riddled with peat.

Beatus-bearing
bog swathe

struggling from the hand-made
word slick.

Hare

on a printing of Horace by Simon de Colines (1480 –1546)

I bought that antic hare of yours today,
A chilblained bouquin in sheep's clothing, Simon.
The vellum had frosted alright, but that italic
Really cuts a dash with austere columns
Enclosing the titled romanitas
Your scrofula-ridden readers dreamed of –
This print's too small even for my slack eye,
But half of ye were blind by forty
So let's incline to workaday metal
Pocking our senses like a felon stung
With rosy judicial irons, while with a pop
Somewhere at the spine Horatian odes

Upturn their swaying tumblers of pure line
To praise your hare's prints, Simon de Colines.

Broom Squires

I

This sign stops the mouth
Of a Punch Bowl letter box:
'No post, birds nesting.'

II

Autumn on the scarp:
Tarmacadam textures veined
With fern and birch sap.

III

The dell conjures you,
Bent double on your birch broom,
Sweeping roads away.

Pastourelle

after Kit Marlowe

If you become a WAV-file, darling, I
will settle in the sound cloud's noisy haze
and watch your data trails criss-cross our sky
heedless of hackers and their canny ways

with complex passwords or double encryption.
Come live with me, beloved. Let us dwell
near pyramids of fractals no Egyptian
could possibly unscramble. Let us spell

out every pixel of our high res passion
within the stanzas of this pastourelle.
So if you'll be an eel, I'll be the trout
that knows your codes, but never locks you out.

Hatchment

The word itself will drop one day —
fade out losing its diamond edge,
retreating like the gauntlet that once lay
beside this hatchment on the window ledge.

These ancient soundings wither like the sedge
around the lake, or better mountain tarn,
of language, gently dripping down
as tallow in a pricket,

wearing thinner than those disused hassocks
swept out of sight into the thicket
of some meagre lean-to aisle.
Will our descendants simply grow laconic

facing this subtle obsolescence,
our words resounding like Old Church Slavonic
shut off behind an iconostasis?
Of course there is still pleasure in eclipse,

expressed by Larkin through the cycle-clips
unfastened in an empty nave.
And yet beyond lies wordlessness
of one who lifts a mildewed rug

to glimpse a mitred brass
or stares for hours into a whitewashed wall
to heal a wounded cross.

At the Burning of Sappho's Poems, A.D. 1073

Flames wave
like dark curls loosened
by island girls.
Each rounded ink-trace

slipping free with carnal sighs,
tongues of light
tease the margins
of taut calf skin.

Sappho is ablaze:
her off-shore lips
sizzling and spitting
into albed laps.

Charred strophes settle
on amice and dalmatic,
while sparrows scatter
to their moonlit roosts.

Digital Detox

I want to make for Michel de Montaigne's tower;
though unsure of its exact location
(because you can't rely on current apps)
I think it's near Bordeaux.

And when I find myself there I'll retrace
all those exotic maxims
(and maybe some mannerist flourishes)
the Renaissance essayist daubed on roof-beams

for the confounding of millennials.
And I'm minded to sing, and seal love letters
to the timbre of a 3D-printed lute.

And later, descending unsteady trip-stairs,
I'll head to the Gironde to wash all taste
for algorithms from my clouded feet.

In Her Flashy Flip-flops ...
a version of Anacreon's fragment 358

One knowing flicker of his golden hair
and the God of Love comes clattering down

with – of all things – a russet beach-ball,
calling me out to play catch with some young one.

In her flashy flip-flops she's as well put together
as a temple on Lesbos, yet she's noticed

my own grey streaks so I haven't a chance
as her footwork stirs the next woman to dance.

Collider

There won't be much to see,
    no Dido or Persephone
        to open gates of horn.

        Only one spur for going down
            with hadron quick-step to the ivory
            underworlds:

                a chance to fling
                    back half-life from the subatomic
                    spring.

My Tongue
after the Old Irish Instructions of King Cormac

When I was young
   I'd watch out for the thrum of stars,
      breathe in the wooded silence round my head.

            High on the hedge of childhood
                  – shy of boundaries – the riverbed
                        seduced my tongue to what I've left half said.

Independence

At six o'clock one August evening we
slipped over the kitchen window sill

to a cracked terrace where the gardener
had been off duty since Independence.

No snipers in the rhododendron beds
observed our Calabrese liquorice

aperitif, no Crossley tenders pitched
down terraces from Montenotte.

By midnight there was little need for caution
in downing alcohol. Just two of us

untended in a Cork garden,
kowtowing to the postcolonial ferns.

Measures for Blind Bishop Fox (c.1448–1528)

Because you were that sort of prelate,
greedy to keep pace equally
with the seven heavens
and the seven joys of Our Lady:
those prime movers in assistive design
(your craftsmen at Farnham) styled
shallow flights of seven steps

with seven paces between each flight
so that you might ascend
and descend like angels
on Jacob's ladder without losing
your footing. Now I'm lifting these measures
(blind bishop) because I'm that sort of poet,
greedy to keep pace equally

with the seven deadly sins
and the seven last words of Christ
from the cross, and ravenous
for your rise from deer park to chapel
where you will raise
ringed hands flushing
with the tang of game.

To Orpheus
translated from Rilke's Sonnette an Orpheus

O how this tree is risking its crisp height,
While Orpheus sings in the ear's high bower
And all grew hushed; but even in that hush
Rose new creations, blinking into light.

Beasts from this stillness, drawn out from the bright
Unfettered forest, from their dens and lairs
Close in together without guile or pain
And softly with receptive ears remain.

Their ragings, roarings, raspings ceased in hearts transfixed.
Here even barest wattle would resound,
A dwelling-house from darkest wishes wound.
Orpheus makes the gate posts tremble
And from the inner ear constructs his temple.

Dinogad's Housecoat

a version of Pais Dinogad, an early medieval Welsh lullaby

Dinogad's housecoat –
Hear how I cut it –
Calls in its stoat-snug pelt:
'Wish, whist, whither.'

Dinogad's housecoat –
See how I spun it –
Finer than the eight tongues
Of slaves bound, yet singing.

So when your daddy, hush Dinogad,
Struck out hunting club and spear
Set to work briskly
From hand and shoulder.

How your father's dogs snapped:
'Gist, grist, gravel'
As papa skewered fish scales
From his tanned coracle

As a lion swipes a tiger moth –
On those fells, too, our stalker snatched
Stag, pig or craggy roe. He'd even snaffle
Dappled upland grouse or a Derwent salmon

Cloaked in a waterfall.
Those beasts your daddy, shush Dinogad,
Splintered with his shrewd point had
No pulse. Whether wild cat

Or boar or fox, they'd need to force
A wing flash as bold
As an eagle's to reel away
From daddy's hunting course.

O Poem

O poem, I want you to mend
the broken glass in the fanlight

of each morning, to have *duende*;
to send groggy parents tumbling

back from school runs to catch you
burgling their maisonettes. I want

lovers to forget each other's names
in the manic flush of reading you,

and I want rush-hour zombies to
rest their heads on your bare shoulders.

Listen, O poem, for the lust
at sundown, to the press of midges

rounding out each dusk. Lend us
to the castanets and vibrant dress

of night. Come out and busk
your way through cocktail hour and salsa class.

O poem, I want you to spend
in light and come back bust.

Coucou
for C. S.

'Coucou' was your last word, playfully scrawled
in the postcard-loving sun,

from the island ironically called
La Réunion.

Come Down So
following a seventh-century Irish prayer

Come down so to reach for us,
perfect centre, gatherer up.

Come to hallow chosen knowing,
come as friend at our frenetic
grazing in elite arenas.

Come freely spoken love,
come silence,
shoaling tacit skeins of wonder –

no halt now for rest in secrets,
hue and cry towards the hidden

turtle doves inside your nest.

I'd Like to Shuffle

I'd like to shuffle like a Saxon village,
perhaps downhill or closer to the stream.
Half a mile or so for better tillage –
a sheltered coppice and a shapely green.
And looking back with unabashed nostalgia
on dappled tower and hollowed-out yew tree,
I'll watch my ancestors streamline their arrows.
I'd like to shuffle like a Saxon, free

from Norman yoke and foreign tyranny.
When all's said and done, I'd like to be
a hollow trackway streaming through the yarrow
half a mile or so beyond the range
of modern signals, fibre-optic seams
beneath me shuffling everything for change.

Lethe

for Mary Murray

Tell me about those summer nights
crouching at the hotel's balustrade
where Paris courted Alexandria.

Cavafy landed poems like so many fish
from a polyglot sea and flapper brides
embraced the Lethe of each cocktail tray

while casting swags of yellow paper up
for you to stash their plethora of dreams
away in childhood's deepest nets.

The wonder is that you recall the steps,
a child with ninety years left to forget
how Europe danced in Alexandria.

Peccadillo
adapted from the Golden Verses of Pythagoras

First mind the gods – if you're mindful of justice –
with their cloudburst contracts; next those paragons
bristling with missiles, not forgetting more earthy
forces of nature.

Settle your kindness on parents and siblings.
Now draw to yourself friendships founded on virtue,
outrunning all others in honour's sprint heats.
Weigh his words with her works:
then repeat.

And don't let some peccadillo
tempt you to hate.
For power can trip
on the gables of fate.

The North Cork Dawn

Some time after the Smerwick massacre
Edmund Spenser roused the North Cork dawn
from his tower house at Kilcolman.

The river Mulla rose beyond the bawn
through native limestone while her courtier
riveted stanzas to the unchoked stars.

Woke

for Francis Ledwidge

When you pass over the senseless shell holes
that separate *sweet music* from *a bomb,*
all of us are woke (as the young now say)
to the strafing mud in your poet's lung.

Even if all the gas-sick stallions of Meath
gambolled right here in this dugout
not one would conjure your Picardy –
Francis, you breathe

sound horses for us all to tether
to trench-thin air we'll wake together.

The Hanging Baskets
for Carmel

On the way through the hall you turn back
for the rosary beads; not out of piety
but simply because you love beads:

their pressure in the palm a gravity
of garnered sunlight flashing from the dresser.
Your hands are those of a mathematician

working an abacus in old Cordoba,
determining the shape of things unseen
and confident that even if the stars

fall from their courses every bead will store
the gathered coolness of a blue mosque's wall
or stir the hanging baskets at your windows.

Skydiver

These days every D-Day veteran is a skydiver.
As he falls I think of all those chaps
with their slick tales of Gold Beach and Anzio,
how Clifford dodged that stick of bombs beneath the chassis

of his armoured car at Monte Cassino,
or of the trusting fellow who hid from shrapnel
under a church door, while his friend bivouacked
behind the safe door of a front-line bank.

As our skydiver's parachute unfurls I'm thinking also
about a soldier in the Great War my grandmother
spoke of, who ran for it when a shell exploded
but then, fearful of firing squads, ran back

as if, he said, doing his exercise. He lands
while journalists' flashbulbs coruscate.
The skydiver says: 'That was bloody marvellous.
Let's do it again.'

The Night I Spoke Irish in Surrey

The night I spoke Irish in Surrey
it was so fluent you'd be wanting
to cut out my tongue.
English words were mistier then

than the cliff path at Dunquin
and Irish was blacker and more attractive
than the black holes waiting
light years above Coolea.

It wasn't the sort of Irish
you'd hear on the news
or in the snack-bar of a railway carriage.
It was pure, unadulterated, Surrey Irish.

When they heard it, all the poets
from Shalford to Virginia Water
sang supple *dindsenchas*
recording everything of note

from the Mole Valley to the Hog's Back:
a bullaun stone at Godalming,
the high cross at Shere
and road bowling at Newlands Corner.

My vocabulary was wider than the Bay of Biscay,
my syntax as crafted as a Galway hooker.
I used the vocative in all the right places
and the dative with archaic precision.

The night I spoke Irish in Surrey
the women of Albury fainted,
the Waverley brewers were sozzled
and matchmakers rejoiced.

Next day we straggled out
over Waterloo Bridge –
the English jangling
in our sorry heads.